www.osha.gov

I0482976

# Hazard Communication Guidance for
# Combustible Dusts

U.S. Department of Labor

Occupational Safety and Health Administration

OSHA 3371-08
2009

# Contents

# Introduction

Combustible dusts are fine particles that present an explosion hazard when suspended in air under certain conditions. A dust explosion can cause catastrophic loss of life, injuries, and destruction of buildings. The U.S. Chemical Safety and Hazard Investigation Board (CSB) identified 281 combustible dust incidents between 1980 and 2005 that led to the deaths of 119 workers, injured 718, and extensively damaged numerous industrial facilities. More recently, additional incidents have occurred. On February 7, 2008, a sugar dust explosion and subsequent fire at a sugar refinery in Port Wentworth, Georgia, caused 14 deaths and left many other workers seriously injured with severe burns.

In many of these incidents, workers and managers were unaware of the potential for dust explosions, or failed to recognize the serious nature of dust explosion hazards. The CSB reviewed Material Safety Data Sheets (MSDS) of 140 known substances that produce combustible dusts and found poor or inadequate transmittal of information regarding potential dust hazards; 41% of the MSDSs reviewed by the CSB did not warn users about potential explosion hazards. Of the remaining 59% of MSDSs sampled, most of the information was either not stated in a place or manner clearly recognized by workers, or was not specific to hazards related to combustible dusts (CSB, 2006).[1]

The Hazard Communication Standard comprehensively addresses the evaluation of the potential hazards of chemicals and the communication of hazard information to workers (29 CFR 1910. 1200(a)(2)). It is a performance-oriented standard that applies to any chemical known to be present in the workplace in such a manner that workers may be exposed under normal conditions of use or in a foreseeable emergency (29 CFR 1910.1200 (b)(2)). Regarding dusts and other particulates, a

[1] Investigation Report No. 2006-H-1 *Combustible Dust Hazard Study.*

3

hazard evaluation must be conducted taking into consideration all discernible hazards, including that of explosibility. It is incumbent upon manufacturers and importers to provide information on the potential for and control of combustible dusts. (See *CPL 02-02-038 Inspection Procedures for the Hazard Communication Standard* (updated in 1998); *CPL 03-00-008 Combustible Dust National Emphasis Program* and letters of interpretation (Mattingly, 1986; English, 1987)).

This document is intended to help manufacturers and importers of chemicals recognize the potential for dust explosions and to identify appropriate protective measures as part of their hazard determination under the Hazard Communication Standard (HCS). This evaluation of hazards ensures that downstream employers and workers are provided MSDSs with complete and accurate information regarding dust explosion hazards, appropriate information is included on labels, and that workers are properly trained regarding workplace combustible dust hazards. Adequate communication of hazard information is essential to ensuring that both employers and workers are aware of dust-related hazards and measures that can be taken to prevent dust explosions.

## OSHA's Hazard Communication Standard

The purpose of the HCS is to ensure that the hazards of all chemicals produced or imported are evaluated and that information concerning their hazards is transmitted to employers and workers.

The HCS has three main components:

- First, **chemical manufacturers and importers** must review available scientific evidence concerning the physical and health hazards of the chemicals they produce or import to determine if they are hazardous (Paragraph (d)). This is called a hazard determination or hazard evaluation;

4

- Second, for every chemical found to be hazardous, the **chemical manufacturer or importer** must develop MSDSs and container labels to be transmitted to downstream users of the chemicals. **Employers** are required to maintain an MSDS in the workplace for each hazardous chemical that they use (Paragraphs (f), (g));

- Third, **all employers** must develop a written hazard communication program and provide information and training to workers about the hazardous chemicals in their workplace (Paragraphs (e), (h)).

The information components of this program – labels, MSDSs, and employee training – are all essential to the effective functioning of a hazard communication program.

## Identifying and Controlling the Potential for Dust Explosions

The hazard determination must include an assessment of all physical and health hazards. The chemical manufacturer or importer must consider the potential exposures that **may occur under normal conditions of use or in foreseeable emergencies**, and address known hazards on the MSDS and, where appropriate, on the label prepared for the product. Regarding combustible dusts, anticipated types of operations, uses or downstream material processing that generate dusts should be considered **normal conditions of use** of a substance. These include operations and uses such as abrasive blasting, cutting, grinding, polishing or crushing of materials; conveying, mixing, sifting or screening dry materials; and the buildup of dried residue from processing wet materials. The CSB found that many of the MSDSs did not identify the potential for combustible dust explosions that could reasonably have been anticipated during downstream material processing (CSB, 2006).

## Examples of dust explosions under normal conditions of use

Example 1: Plastic pellets shipped from a polyethylene plant rarely pose a combustible dust hazard until they are processed downstream where they produce dust particles. In 1991 in Littleton, New Hampshire an employee was injured due to a dust explosion while he was feeding 400 pounds of granular polyalphamethyl styrene (CAS 25014-31-7) through a micropulverizer (equipped with a .032-inch screen) into a dust collector. The dust collector had no provision for explosion relief or venting. Apparently, a piece of metal got past the magnet in the micropulverizer, ignited the dust in the system, and caused a fire and explosion that blew open the access door to the dust collector.

Example 2: An aqueous solution of a combustible dust material can dry to produce combustible dust. In 2003 in Kinston, North Carolina 6 people were killed and more than 30 others were injured due to an explosion caused by the buildup of dust above suspended ceilings generated from the drying process of aqueous polyethene solution during the production of rubber stoppers.

Source: CSB, Dust Incident Data Files

Combustible dust is defined as a solid material composed of distinct particles or pieces, regardless of size, shape, or chemical composition, which presents a fire or deflagration hazard when suspended in air or some other oxidizing medium over a range of concentrations. Combustible dusts are often either organic or metal dusts that are finely ground into very small particles, fibers, fines, chips, chunks, flakes, or a small mixture of these. As discussed in OSHA's Safety and Health Information Bulletin (SHIB): *Combustible Dust in Industry: Preventing and Mitigating the Effects of*

*Fire and Explosions* (www.osha.gov/dts/shib/ shib073105.html), dust particles with an effective diameter of less than 420 microns (those passing through a U.S. No. 40 standard sieve) should be deemed to meet the criterion of the definition. However, larger particles can still pose a deflagration hazard (for instance, as larger particles are moved, they can abrade each other, creating smaller particles). In addition, particles can stick together (agglomerate) due to electrostatic charges accumulated through handling, causing them to become explosible when dispersed. Types of dusts include, but are not limited to: metal dust, such as aluminum and magnesium; wood dust; plastic or rubber dust; biosolids; coal dust; organic dust, such as flour, sugar, paper, soap, and dried blood; and dusts from certain textiles. OSHA's *Combustible Dust* poster provides examples of products or materials from which combustible dust explosions could occur if they are processed in powdered form. This poster can be accessed at www.osha.gov/Publications/ combustibledustposter.pdf.

Five elements are necessary to initiate a dust explosion, often referred to as the "Dust Explosion Pentagon".[2]

The first three elements are those needed for a fire, i.e., the familiar "fire triangle":

1. Combustible dust (fuel);
2. Ignition source (heat); and,
3. Oxygen in air (oxidizer).

An additional two elements must be present for a combustible dust explosion:

4. Dispersion of dust particles in sufficient quantity and concentration; and,
5. Confinement of the dust cloud.

If one of the above five elements is missing, an explosion cannot occur.

[2] OSHA Fact Sheet, (March 2008), Hazard Alert:*Combustible Dust Explosions.*

An initial (primary) dust explosion in processing equipment may shake loose accumulated dust, or damage a containment system (such as a duct, vessel, or collector). This causes the dust to become airborne and this additional airborne dust, if ignited, may cause one or more secondary explosions. These can be more destructive than a primary explosion due to the increased quantity and concentration of dispersed combustible dust and the larger ignition source.

The ease of ignition and the severity of a combustible dust explosion are typically influenced by particle size. Other factors that influence the explosiveness of dusts include moisture content, ambient humidity, oxygen available for combustion, the shape of dust particles, and the concentration of dust in the air. Physical properties used to measure combustible dusts include:

- MIE, the minimum ignition energy, which predicts the ease and likelihood of ignition of a dispersed dust cloud.

- MEC, the minimum explosible concentration, which measures the minimum amount of dust dispersed in air required to spread an explosion. (The MEC is analogous to the Lower Flammable Limit (LFL) or Lower Explosive Limit (LEL) for gases and vapors in air).

- $K_{st}$, the dust deflagration index, measures the **relative** explosion severity compared to other dusts. The larger the value for $K_{st}$, the more

**Examples of $K_{st}$ Values for Different Types of Dusts**

| Dust explosion class* | $K_{st}$ (bar.m/s)* | Characteristic* |
|---|---|---|
| St 0 | 0 | No explosion |
| St 1 | >0 and ≤ 200 | Weak explosion |
| St 2 | >200 and ≤ 300 | Strong explosion |
| St 3 | >300 | Very strong explosion |

The actual class is sample specific and will depend on varying characteristics of the material such as particle size or moisture.

\* OSHA CPL 03-00-008 - *Combustible Dust National Emphasis Program.*
\*\* NFPA 68, *Standard on Explosion Prevention by Deflagration Venting.*

8

severe the explosion (See Table, below). $K_{st}$ provides the best "single number" estimate of the anticipated behavior of a dust deflagration.

Different dusts of the same chemical material can have different ignitability and explosibility characteristics, depending upon physical characteristics such as particle size, shape, and moisture content. These physical characteristics can change during manufacturing, use or while the material is being processed. Any combustible dust with a $K_{st}$ value greater than zero can be subject to dust deflagration. Even weak explosions can cause significant damage, injury and death. For example, sugar has a relatively low $K_{st}$ but it fueled a tragic explosion in 2008 that killed 14 workers.

Specific guidance measures to prevent explosions can be found in OSHA's SHIB *Combustible Dust in Industry: Preventing and Mitigating the Effects of Fire and Explosions*, which lists measures to control dusts, eliminate ignition sources, and limit the effects of explosions to minimize injuries. Initial preventative steps are to contain combustible dust to areas that are properly designed and located, with ignition sources either eliminated or controlled. Equipment or spaces such as ducts, dust collectors, vessels, and processing equipment that contain combustible dust should be designed in a manner to prevent leaks to minimize the escape of dust into work areas. Any dust that settles on workplace surfaces

| Typical material** |
| --- |
| Silica |
| Powdered milk, charcoal, sulfur, sugar and zinc |
| Cellulose, wood flour, and poly methyl acrylate |
| Anthraquinone, aluminum, and magnesium |
| |

should be removed through a routinely imple-
mented housekeeping program. Areas or equipment potentially subject to explosions, including
the dust collection system, should also be
designed to relieve pressure in a safe manner, or
be provided with proper suppression, explosion
prevention systems, or an oxygen-deficient
atmosphere.

## MSDS Preparation

The HCS requires chemical manufacturers and
importers to develop an MSDS for each hazardous
chemical they produce or import. Chemical manufacturers and importers must provide any generally applicable precautions for safe handling and
use on the MSDS (29 CFR 1910.1200(g)(2)(viii)).
They must also determine generally applicable
control measures such as appropriate engineering
controls, work practices, or personal protective
equipment, and include that information on the
MSDS (29 CFR 1910.1200(g)(2)(ix)). Employers, in
turn, must retain an MSDS in the workplace for
each hazardous chemical that they use and ensure
that MSDSs are readily accessible to workers.

MSDSs provide comprehensive hazard information, and serve as the key reference document
for exposed workers and others, such as health
professionals providing services to those workers.
New information regarding chemical hazards or
protective measures must be added to the MSDS
when the preparer becomes aware of this information. Updating MSDSs will provide employers
and workers with the most current information
needed to understand the hazards associated with
combustible dusts, as well as appropriate protective measures to be taken. Dissemination of this
updated information is also critical to reduce
exposures to combustible dusts, which have been
associated with multiple incidents.

The following MSDS requirements are applicable to combustible dust hazards:

- The chemical and common name(s) of the hazardous chemical or the chemical and common names of all ingredients which have been determined to present a physical hazard when present in a mixture (1910.1200(g)(2)(i) (C)(1));

- Physical and chemical characteristics of the hazardous chemical (for example, vapor pressure or flash point) including the potential for fire, explosion, and reactivity (if known, $K_{st}$, MIE, MEC and particle size are combustible dust characteristics) (1910.1200(2)(g)(ii) and (iii));

- Any generally applicable precautions for safe handling and use, which are known to the chemical manufacturer, importer or employer preparing the MSDS, including appropriate hygienic practices, protective measures during repair and maintenance of contaminated equipment, and procedures for cleanup of spills and leaks (1910.1200(g)(2)(viii)); and

- Any generally applicable control measures, which are known to the chemical manufacturer, importer or employer preparing the MSDS, such as appropriate engineering controls, work practices, or personal protective equipment (1910.1200(g)(2)(ix)).

## Examples of combustible dust warning information on the MSDS
### (Presented in the ANSI (Z400.1) Format)

Section 2. Hazard Identification:

<u>Emergency Overview</u>

**WARNING! MAY FORM COMBUSTIBLE DUST CONCENTRATIONS IN AIR (DURING PROCESSING)**

Section 5. Fire Fighting Measures:

**Explosion**: Avoid generating dust; fine dust dispersed in air in sufficient concentrations, and in the presence of an ignition source is a potential dust explosion hazard.

Section 6. Accidental Release Measures:

Dust Deposits should not be allowed to accumulate on surfaces, as these may form an explosive mixture if they are released into the atmosphere in sufficient concentration.

Avoid dispersal of dust in the air (i.e., clearing dust surfaces with compressed air).

Nonsparking tools should be used.

Section 7. Handling and Storage:

Minimize dust generation and accumulation.

Routine housekeeping should be instituted to ensure that dusts do not accumulate on surfaces.

Dry powders can build static electricity charges when subjected to the friction of transfer and mixing operations. Provide adequate precautions, such as electrical grounding and bonding, or inert atmospheres.

Section 8. Exposure controls/personal protection:

It is recommended that all dust control equipment such as local exhaust ventilation and material transport systems involved in handling of this product contain explosion relief vents or an explosion suppression system or an oxygen-deficient environment.

Ensure that dust-handling systems (such as exhaust ducts, dust collectors, vessels, and processing equipment) are designed in a manner to prevent the escape of dust into the work area (i.e., there is no leakage from the equipment).

Use only appropriately classified electrical equipment and powered industrial trucks:

Section 16. Other Information

Refer to NFPA 654, *Standard for the Prevention of Fire and Dust Explosions from the Manufacturing, Processing, and Handling of Combustible Particulate Solids*, for safe handling.[3]

[3] NFPA 654 is one of several potential references that discuss preventative measures for combustible dusts. Please see the references section, below, for additional resources.

# Product Labels

Containers of material with HCS physical and health hazards are subject to the labeling requirements of the HCS (29 CFR 1910.1200(f)). Manufacturers, importers and distributors are required to assess available evidence regarding a product's hazards and must consider exposures under normal conditions of use or in foreseeable emergencies when evaluating what hazards must appear on the label. Where manufacturers are aware that the downstream use of their product routinely generates combustible dusts, a warning addressing a potential explosion hazard should be included on the label as an immediate visual reminder.

The HCS requires that manufacturers and employers determine and provide appropriate hazard warning language for labels. As discussed in *CPL 02-02-038 - CPL 2-2.38D - Inspection Procedures for the Hazard Communication Standard,* the label is intended to be an immediate visual reminder of the hazards of a chemical. It is not necessary, however, that every hazard presented by a chemical be listed on the label. The MSDS is used for this purpose. Manufacturers, importers and distributors will have to assess the evidence regarding the product's hazards and must consider exposures under normal conditions of use or in foreseeable emergencies when evaluating what hazard warnings must be listed on the label.

**An example of combustible dust warning information on a label:**

> **Warning: May Form Combustible (Explosive) Dust - Air Mixtures**
>
> Keep away from all ignition sources including heat, sparks and flame.
>
> Keep container closed and grounded.
>
> Prevent dust accumulations to minimize explosion hazard.

## Training and Information

The purpose of the HCS is to provide information so that workers and employers can take the appropriate steps to protect themselves. When workers are trained to recognize and prevent hazards they can be instrumental in recognizing unsafe conditions, taking preventative action, and/or alerting management.

The HCS requires employers to inform workers about the general requirements of the standard, operations where hazardous chemicals are present, and the location of the written HCS program, MSDSs, and hazardous chemical inventory (29 CFR 1910.1200(h)(2)).

In addition, employers are required to specifically train workers in the methods used to detect the presence or release of a hazardous chemical, the physical and health hazards of the chemical, and control measures (including work practices, emergency procedures, and personal protective equipment) (29 CFR 1910.1200(h)(3)).

The first two components of the HCS (evaluation of hazards and provision of hazard information via labels and MSDSs) provide the foundation for the worker training. The MSDSs/labels provide the necessary baseline information for worker training regarding physical and health hazards, personal protective equipment, and emergency procedures. Employers who use materials capable of producing combustible dusts must evaluate those operations and tasks where dusts are present or may be generated and provide the required information and training to workers.

## Additional Information

In order to focus attention on combustible dust hazards and promote awareness, OSHA has undertaken several initiatives. The agency has reissued the Combustible Dust National Emphasis

Program (NEP) Instruction (2008); developed a Combustible Dust Fact Sheet and poster, a Safety and Health Information Bulletin (*Combustible Dust in Industry: Preventing and Mitigating the Effects of Fire and Explosions*) and a Combustible Dust Safety and Health Topics web page (www.osha. gov/ dsg/combustibledust/index.html). In addition, OSHA's Combustible Dust NEP will increase enforcement activities and focus on specific industry groups that have experienced frequent combustible dust incidents.

# References

## OSHA

Combustible Dust Safety and Health Topics Page (www.osha.gov/dsg/combustibledust/index.html):

- Combustible Dust National Emphasis Program Instruction, OSHA Directive CPL 03-00-008, (2008).
- Safety and Health Information Bulletin (SHIB) (07-31-2005) *Combustible Dust in Industry: Preventing and Mitigating the Effects of Fire and Explosions.*
- OSHA Fact Sheet, (March 2008), *Hazard Alert: Combustible Dust Explosions.*
- OSHA Poster (2008), *Combustible Dust.*

**Applicable OSHA requirements include:**

- General Duty Clause, Section 5(a)(1) of the *Occupational Safety and Health Act* (Employers must keep workplaces free from recognized hazards likely to cause death or serious physical harm).
- §1910.22 General requirements (See Housekeeping)
- §1910.38 Emergency action plans
- §1910.39 Fire prevention plans
- §1910.94 Ventilation
- §1910.157 Portable fire extinguishers
- §1910.178 Powered industrial trucks
- §1910.269 Electric Power generation, transmission and distribution (See Coal and ash handling)

- §1910.272 Grain handling facilities
- §1910.307 Hazardous (classified) locations
- §1910.1200 Hazard Communication

**Letters of Interpretation:**

Jan. 16, 1986 - *Application of the Hazard Communication standard to a nuisance particulate*, Honorable Mack Mattingly.

November 20, 1987 - *Applicability of the revised Hazard Communication Standard to the grain industry*, Honorable Glenn English.

**ANSI:**

- ANSI Z129.1 American National Standard for Hazardous Industrial Chemicals - Precautionary Labeling
- ANSI Z400.1 American National Standard for Hazardous Industrial Chemicals – Material Safety Data Sheets – Preparation

**U.S. Chemical Safety and Hazard Investigation Board:**

Investigation Report No. 2006-H-1 Combustible Dust Hazard Study, November 2006.

Dust Incident Data File at www.csb.gov.

**The primary National Fire Protection Association consensus standards and documents related to this hazard (see www.nfpa.org to view NFPA standards):**

- NFPA 61, Standard for the Prevention of Fires and Dust Explosions in Agricultural and Food Processing Facilities
- NFPA 68, Standard on Explosion Protection by Deflagration Venting
- NFPA 69, Standard on Explosion Prevention Systems
- NFPA 484, Standard for Combustible Metals
- NFPA 499, Recommended Practice for the Classification of Combustible Dusts and of Hazardous (Classified) Locations for Electrical Installations in Chemical Process Areas
- NFPA 654, Standard for the Prevention of Fire and Dust Explosions from the Manufacturing, Processing, and Handling of Combustible

Particulate Solids

- NFPA 655, Standard for the Prevention of Sulfur Fires and Explosions

- NFPA 664, Standard for the Prevention of Fires and Explosions in Wood Processing and Woodworking Facilities

- NFPA *Fire Protection Handbook*, 19th Edition

**Other:**

FM 7-76, "Prevention and Mitigation of Combustible Dust Explosions and Fires," Loss Prevention Data Sheet 7-76. FM Global, 2001.

# OSHA Assistance

OSHA can provide extensive help through a variety of programs, including technical assistance about effective safety and health programs, state plans, workplace consultations, and training and education.

### Safety and Health Program Management System Guidelines

Effective management of worker safety and health protection is a decisive factor in reducing the extent and severity of work-related injuries and illnesses and their related costs. In fact, an effective safety and health management system forms the basis of good worker protection, can save time and money, increase productivity and reduce employee injuries, illnesses and related workers' compensation costs.

To assist employers and workers in developing effective safety and health management systems, OSHA published recommended Safety and Health Program Management Guidelines (54 *Federal Register* (16): 3904-3916, January 26, 1989). These voluntary guidelines can be applied to all places of employment covered by OSHA.

The guidelines identify four general elements critical to the development of a successful safety and health management system:

- Management leadership and worker involvement,

- Worksite analysis,

- Hazard prevention and control, and

- Safety and health training.

The guidelines recommend specific actions, under each of these general elements, to achieve an effective

safety and health management system. The *Federal Register* notice is available online at www.osha.gov.

## State Programs

*The Occupational Safety and Health Act of 1970* (OSH Act) encourages states to develop and operate their own job safety and health plans. OSHA approves and monitors these plans. Twenty-four states, Puerto Rico and the Virgin Islands currently operate approved state plans: 22 cover both private and public (state and local government) employment; Connecticut, New Jersey, New York and the Virgin Islands cover the public sector only. States and territories with their own OSHA-approved occupational safety and health plans must adopt standards identical to, or at least as effective as, the Federal OSHA standards.

## Consultation Services

Consultation assistance is available on request to employers who want help in establishing and maintaining a safe and healthful workplace. Largely funded by OSHA, the service is provided at no cost to the employer. Primarily developed for smaller employers with more hazardous operations, the consultation service is delivered by state governments employing professional safety and health consultants. Comprehensive assistance includes an appraisal of all mechanical systems, work practices, and occupational safety and health hazards of the workplace and all aspects of the employer's present job safety and health program. In addition, the service offers assistance to employers in developing and implementing an effective safety and health program. No penalties are proposed or citations issued for hazards identified by the consultant. OSHA provides consultation assistance to the employer with the assurance that his or her name and firm and any information about the workplace will not be routinely reported to OSHA enforcement staff. For more information concerning consultation assistance, see OSHA's website at www.osha.gov.

## Strategic Partnership Program

OSHA's Strategic Partnership Program helps encourage, assist and recognize the efforts of partners to eliminate serious workplace hazards and achieve a high level of worker safety and health. Most strategic partnerships seek to have a broad impact by

building cooperative relationships with groups of employers and workers. These partnerships are voluntary relationships between OSHA, employers, worker representatives, and others (e.g., trade unions, trade and professional associations, universities, and other government agencies).

For more information on this and other agency programs, contact your nearest OSHA office, or visit OSHA's website at www.osha.gov.

## OSHA Training and Education

OSHA area offices offer a variety of information services, such as technical advice, publications, audiovisual aids and speakers for special engagements. OSHA's Training Institute in Arlington Heights, IL, provides basic and advanced courses in safety and health for Federal and state compliance officers, state consultants, Federal agency personnel, and private sector employers, workers and their representatives.

The OSHA Training Institute also has established OSHA Training Institute Education Centers to address the increased demand for its courses from the private sector and from other federal agencies. These centers are colleges, universities, and non-profit organizations that have been selected after a competition for participation in the program.

OSHA also provides funds to nonprofit organizations, through grants, to conduct workplace training and education in subjects where OSHA believes there is a lack of workplace training. Grants are awarded annually.

For more information on grants, training and education, contact the OSHA Training Institute, Directorate of Training and Education, 2020 South Arlington Heights Road, Arlington Heights, IL 60005, (847) 297-4810, or see Training on OSHA's website at www.osha.gov. For further information on any OSHA program, contact your nearest OSHA regional office listed at the end of this publication.

## Information Available Electronically

OSHA has a variety of materials and tools available on its website at www.osha.gov. These include electronic tools, such as *Safety and Health Topics*, *eTools*, *Expert Advisors*; regulations, directives and publications; videos and other information for employers and workers. OSHA's software programs and eTools

walk you through challenging safety and health issues and common problems to find the best solutions for your workplace.

## OSHA Publications

OSHA has an extensive publications program. For a listing of free items, visit OSHA's website at www.osha.gov or contact the OSHA Publications Office, U.S. Department of Labor, 200 Constitution Avenue, NW, N-3101, Washington, DC 20210; telephone (202) 693-1888 or fax to (202) 693-2498.

## Contacting OSHA

To report an emergency, file a complaint, or seek OSHA advice, assistance, or products, call (800) 321-OSHA or contact your nearest OSHA Regional or Area office listed below. The teletypewriter (TTY) number is (877) 889-5627.

Written correspondence can be mailed to the nearest OSHA Regional or Area Office listed below or to OSHA's national office at: U.S. Department of Labor, Occupational Safety and Health Administration, 200 Constitution Avenue, N.W., Washington, DC 20210.

By visiting OSHA's website at www.osha.gov, you can also:

- File a complaint online;
- Submit general inquires about workplace safety and health electronically; and
- Find more information about OSHA and occupational safety and health.

# OSHA Regional Offices

**Region I**
(CT,* ME, MA, NH, RI, VT*)
JFK Federal Building, Room E340
Boston, MA 02203
(617) 565-9860

**Region II**
(NJ,* NY,* PR,* VI*)
201 Varick Street, Room 670
New York, NY 10014
(212) 337-2378

**Region III**
(DE, DC, MD,* PA, VA,* WV)
The Curtis Center
170 S. Independence Mall West, Suite 740 West
Philadelphia, PA 19106-3309
(215) 861-4900

**Region IV**
(AL, FL, GA, KY,* MS, NC,* SC,* TN*)
61 Forsyth Street, SW, Room 6T50
Atlanta, GA 30303
(404) 562-2300

**Region V**
(IL, IN,* MI,* MN,* OH, WI)
230 South Dearborn Street, Room 3244
Chicago, IL 60604
(312) 353-2220

**Region VI**
(AR, LA, NM,* OK, TX)
525 Griffin Street, Room 602
Dallas, TX 75202
(972) 850-4145

**Region VII**
(IA,* KS, MO, NE)
Two Pershing Square
2300 Main Street, Suite 1010
Kansas City, MO 64108-2416
(816) 283-8745

**Region VIII**
(CO, MT, ND, SD, UT,* WY*)
1999 Broadway, Suite 1690
PO Box 46550
Denver, CO 80202-5716
(720) 264-6550

**Region IX**
(AZ,* CA,* HI,* NV,* and American Samoa,
Guam and the Northern Mariana Islands)
90 7th Street, Suite 18-100
San Francisco, CA 94103
(415) 625-2547

**Region X**
(AK,* ID, OR,* WA*)
1111 Third Avenue, Suite 715
Seattle, WA 98101-3212
(206) 553-5930

* These states and territories operate their own OSHA-approved job safety and health programs and cover state and local government workers as well as private sector personnel. The Connecticut, New Jersey, New York and Virgin Islands plans cover public employees only. States with approved programs must have standards that are identical to, or at least as effective as, the Federal OSHA standards.

Note: To get contact information for OSHA area offices, OSHA-approved State Plans, and OSHA Consultation Projects, please visit us online at www.osha.gov or call us at 1-800-321-OSHA (6742).